Egg to Penguin

Camilla de la Bédoyère

QED Publishing

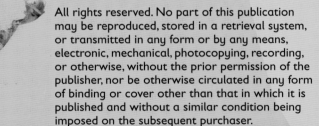

Words in **bold** are explained in the Glossary on page 22.

Copyright © QED Publishing 2011

First published in the UK in 2011 by
QED Publishing
A Quarto Group company
226 City Road
London EC1V 2TT

www.qed-publishing.co.uk

A catalogue record for this book is available
from the British Library.

ISBN 978 1 84835 577 4

Printed in China

Editor Alexandra Koken
Designer and Picture Researcher Melissa Alaverdy

Picture credits
(t=top, b=bottom, l=left, r=right, c=centre)

Alamy 6t Wayne Lynch/All Canada Photos

Corbis 9c Kevin Schafer, 12t Frans Lanting, 22-23 Fritz Polking/Frank Lane Picture Agency

Getty 6b Rosemary Calvert, 8 Joseph van Os, 9t Kevin Schafer/Peter Arnold Images, 10 David Tipling, 20l Bill Curtsinger, 20-21 Paul McKenzie

Nature PL 10 Pete Oxford, 11c and 16tl Fred Oliver, 16br Solvin Zankl

Shutterstock back cover Gentoo Multimedia Ltd, 1b Jan Martin Will, 2tl Viki&Maki, 2tr Galina Barsky, 3t Spyder, 5tr Jan Martin Will, 5tl Mboe, 24 arbit

Photolibrary front cover Thorsten Milse,/Picture Press 1t Konrad Wothe/Oxford Scientific, 4 Wayne Lynch/All Canada Photo, 5b Wolfgang bechtolhold/imagebroker.net, 7 Juniors Bildarchiv, 11 Don Paulson/ Superstock, 12c Wayne Lynch, 13 Gerald Lacz/Peter Arnold Images, 14 Frank Krahmer/Cusp, 12tl and 12 tr Doug Cheeseman/Peter Arnold Images, 17l and 17r Thorsten Milse, 18-19 Konrad Wothe/Oxford Scientific, 19 Tui De Roy/Oxford Scientific, 24 kp Wolf/ Picture Press

Contents

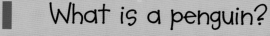

What is a penguin? 4

The story of a penguin 6

The colony 8

Laying an egg 10

The long walk 12

Welcome home 14

The egg hatches 16

Chicks together 18

Growing up 20

Glossary 22

Index 23

Notes for parents and teachers . . 24

What is a penguin?

Penguins are birds, but they cannot fly. All birds have feathers and a beak, and they lay eggs.

Most birds use their feathers and wings to fly. Penguins use their feathers to keep warm. They use their wings, or flippers, to swim.

beak

⇦ A penguin's wings are too small for flying. They are called flippers.

flipper

feet

4

Penguins live in cold places.
They hunt fish to eat.

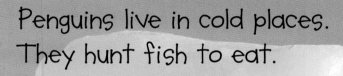

⇨ Little blue penguins are just 35 centimetres tall. Emperor penguins are more than 1 metre tall.

crest

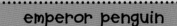

emperor penguin

⇦ Royal penguins have yellow feathers on their head. These feathers are called a crest.

The story of a penguin

Emperor penguins live in big groups called **colonies**. Their home is the **Antarctic**, which is at the bottom of our planet Earth.

A mother penguin lays one egg at the beginning of winter. The father looks after the egg.

When the egg is ready, it opens and a baby penguin comes out.

Baby penguins are called chicks.

chick

⇧ Penguin chicks do not look like their parents.

⇦ The mother penguin lays only one egg at a time.

egg

The story of how an egg grows into an adult penguin is called a **life cycle**.

adult

3

⇧ Male and female emperor penguins look the same.

The colony

At the start of winter, emperor penguins meet on sheets of ice to **mate**. The weather is cold.

Males and females call each other. The sound they make is called a **bray**.

⇧ Every penguin in the colony makes a different bray.

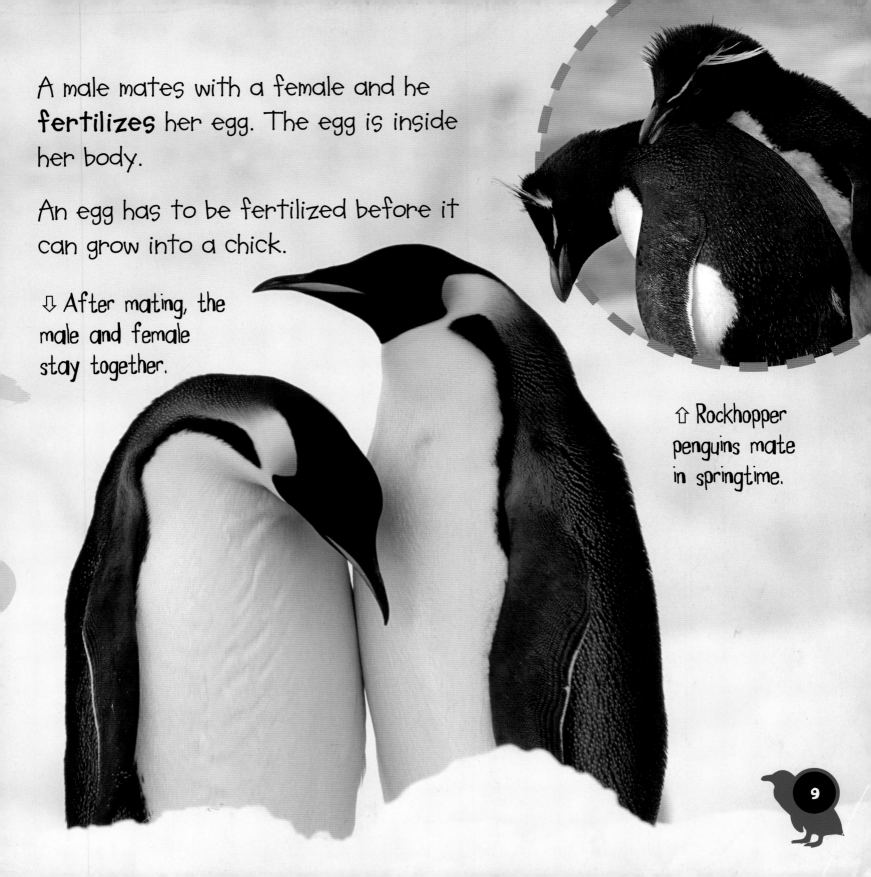

A male mates with a female and he **fertilizes** her egg. The egg is inside her body.

An egg has to be fertilized before it can grow into a chick.

⇩ After mating, the male and female stay together.

⇧ Rockhopper penguins mate in springtime.

9

Laying an egg

Emperor penguins do not build nests. They carry their eggs instead.

The female lays a single egg on the ice. The male uses his beak to push the egg onto his feet.

The male has a bare patch of skin on his belly. This is called a **brood patch**. He lays this over the egg.

2

brood patch

⇧ The brood patch keeps the egg warm.

1

egg

⇦ The egg has a strong shell on the outside.

⇩ The egg is on the male's feet. Now it will not get too cold.

⇨ Gentoo penguins build a nest for their eggs.

3

11

The long walk

The cold Antarctic winter brings snow and wind. Male penguins huddle together to keep warm.

⇧ The males do not eat while the females are away.

The males look after the eggs and the females walk back to the sea. The long walk takes four weeks.

The female penguins catch lots of fish and fill their stomach with food.

Then, the females begin the long walk back to the colony.

⇩ Penguins often slide on their belly. This is called tobogganing.

⇦ Humboldt penguins hunt in warmer waters.

Welcome home

After feeding, the female walks for four weeks to get back to the colony. She finds her mate by calling him.

⇩ The female penguins walk home.

Now the male can give the egg to the mother. He walks to the sea to find food. He has not eaten for more than two months.

⇨ The male holds the egg on his feet.

⇧ The female takes her egg from the male.

Now it's the female's turn to look after the egg. The egg is about to **hatch**.

The egg hatches

1 The chick breaks out of the shell. It sits on its mother's feet to keep warm.

The mother feeds the chick with food that was in her stomach. The chick is small and fluffy.

⇧ The shell begins to crack open.

2

⇨ The chick comes out of the shell.

16

The father comes back from the sea. He has a stomach full of food.

The parents take it in turns to feed the chick. They keep it warm and safe.

⇑ The parents feed the chick with food from their stomach.

⇨ The chick stays with its parents.

Chicks together

When the chicks are seven weeks old they huddle together. A group of chicks is called a crèche.

Adult penguins take it in turns to look after the crèche.

The other parents walk to the sea. They find fish and **squid** to eat.

As they grow, the chicks get new feathers. Soon they will look like their parents.

⇧ Chicks lose their fluffy feathers. New feathers are growing.

⇦ The chicks stay safe and warm in their crèche.

19

Growing up

Finally, the large chicks have lost all their fluffy feathers. They look like their parents.

The chicks walk to the sea and dive in the water. They can swim and catch fish without any help.

⇨ Young penguins know how to swim. Their parents do not have to teach them.

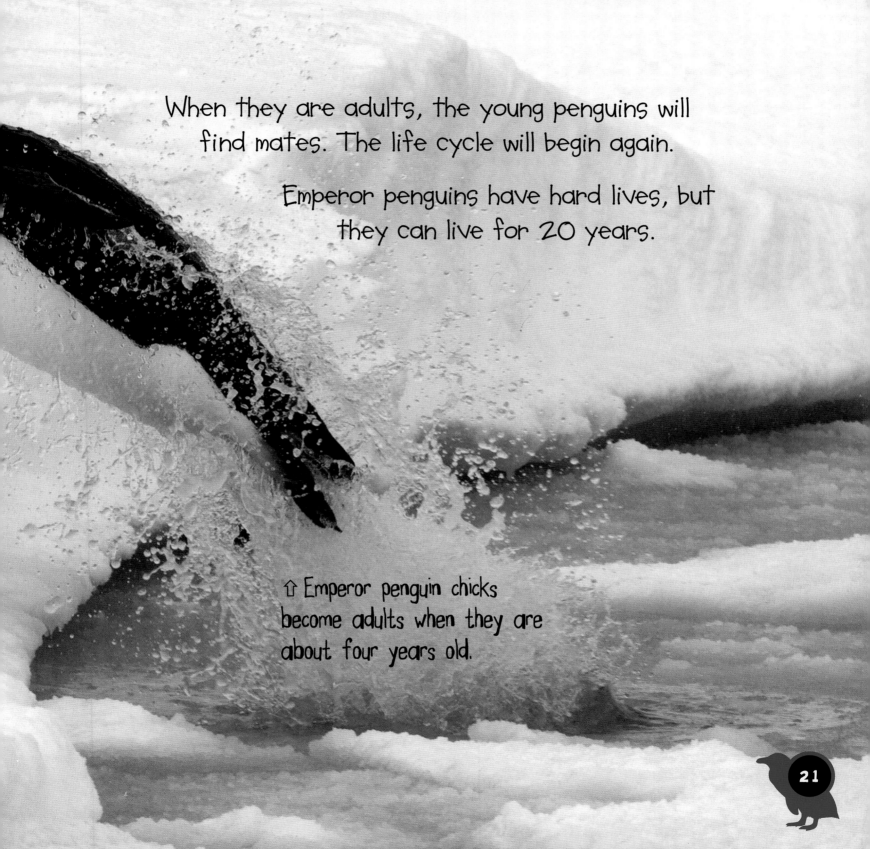

When they are adults, the young penguins will find mates. The life cycle will begin again.

Emperor penguins have hard lives, but they can live for 20 years.

⇧ Emperor penguin chicks become adults when they are about four years old.

Glossary

Antarctic
This is the large area of land around the South Pole. It is a cold place that is covered in ice.

Bray
A penguin's loud call to find its mate.

Brood patch
A patch of bare skin that warms the egg. It is warmer than the penguin's feathers.

Colony
A group of penguins that live together.

Fertilize
When a male fertilizes a female's egg, it can grow into a new living thing.

Hatch
When an egg breaks open and a chick comes out.

Life cycle
The story of how a living thing changes from birth to death and how it produces young.

Mate
When a male fertilizes the female's egg the penguins are mating.

Squid
An animal with a soft body and ten 'arms'. Squid live in the sea.

Index

Antarctic 6, 12, 22

bray 8, 22
brood patch 10, 22

chicks 6, 16, 17, 18–20, 21
colonies 6, 13, 14, 22
crèche 18, 19
crest 5

eggs 4, 6, 9, 10–11, 12, 15, 16
emperor penguin 5, 6–21

feathers 4, 5, 19, 20
fertilized eggs 9, 22
fish 5, 13, 19, 20
flippers 4
food 13, 15, 16, 17

gentoo penguin 11

hatch 15, 16, 22
Humboldt penguin 13
hunting 5, 13

life cycle 7, 21, 22
little blue penguin 5

mating 8–9, 22

nests 11

rockhopper penguin 9
royal penguin 5

squid 19, 22
swimming 4, 20

tobogganing 13

wings 4

Notes for parents and teachers

Look through the book and talk about the pictures. Read the captions and ask questions about the things in the photographs that have not been mentioned in the text.

Explore measurements: use a measuring tape to find out how big emperor penguins are. Use the Internet* to find the sizes of the other penguins that feature in this book. Ask children to draw a picture showing four types of penguin, to show their different sizes.

Penguins have very unusual life cycles. Together, you can explore the life cycles of other birds, such as chickens and garden birds. Find out what other young birds eat.

Remind children that they must never get close to a nest, eggs or hatchlings because the parent bird may abandon a disturbed nest. Find out about other flightless birds.

Penguin chicks need a great deal of care and attention, just like human babies. Talk about what babies are able to do for themselves, and what things adults have to do for them. Think about the ways that babies learn to do things for themselves, and how they change as they grow.

Talking about a child's own family helps them to link the processes of reproduction and growth to their own circumstances. Drawing simple family trees, showing them photographs of themselves as babies and talking to grandparents are all fun ways to engage young children.

*The publishers cannot accept responsibility for information, links, or any other content of Internet sites, or third-party websites.

24